Voting is a way to choose.

You can vote for favorite books, movie stars, candy bars . . . or even puppies!

HOW THE CHRIS SMITH FAMILY VOTED FOR THEIR DOG, ELMER . . .

8 years ago . . .

. . . when I was a puppy at the dog pound, the Smiths came along.

. . . looking for a puppy?

They couldn't decide between me and a poodle so they VOTED.

I vote for the mutt!

No, the poodle! Vote for the poodle, Angela!

Mutt!

But they could have flipped a coin: heads— the mutt; tails— the poodle.

Tails for the poodle! That's not fair!

Why not?

Because TWO people wanted me. Only ONE wanted the poodle!

Voting was the way to find out what the most people wanted—me!

Does that mean one person didn't like you?

Well, you can't please all the people all the time . . . but I think I've grown on her.

So if Chris gets the most votes, she'll be mayor. What does the mayor do?

The mayor is the leader of the city. Let's go help Chris find some votes.

VOTE FOR SMITH

If someone wants to be elected mayor, she needs to convince as many people as possible to vote for her!

Many people just don't vote. Why not?

11

Maybe they think their vote is like a little drop of water in an enormous ocean. Their vote *is* only one out of many, many votes. But sometimes the winner of an election is decided by just a few votes.

Who decided who could vote?

When this country began, the Founding Fathers wrote a constitution. It said how we would govern ourselves. It said people should vote; but it didn't say *who* could vote. That was left to each state to decide. And that was a problem!

Angry people protested. They wrote letters. They held rallies and made speeches. They marched, were arrested, and went on hunger strikes. Some were killed trying to claim their right to vote. But it took many years, four amendments to the Constitution, and several new laws before all citizens, 18 years or older, were allowed to vote.

If you want to vote, you need to register. Where? At your town office. Or you can download a registration form from the Internet, or you might even find a booth set up at a shopping mall or at a political rally.

Do you want to join a political party? You've probably heard of the Democrats and the Republicans. But you could join the Green Party, the Libertarians, the America First Party, or the Progressives, to name just a few. Or you could be independent and not join any party at all.

Before you vote, you'll need to find out about the different candidates. How? Read newspapers, watch TV news, listen to the radio, or surf the Internet. Do you agree with their ideas?

You might have a chance to hear the candidates debate.

You might even be able to ask questions!

Before an election, everyone tries to guess who will win. Pollsters ask some of the voters whom they're planning to vote for. Then they estimate who will be the winner. But voters can change their minds.

How can you help your candidate win? You can volunteer to answer phones, call voters, address envelopes, or hand out flyers. Campaigns need lots of help.

And they need lots of money to help pay for phones, computers, stamps, flyers and bumper stickers, and, most of all, ads and more ads! Where will they find the money?

You might want to donate a few dollars to your favorite candidate's campaign. Or maybe you'll be invited to a fundraising dinner. Would you like to pay $250 for a fancy hamburger and a chance to meet the candidate?

If you donate lots of money, maybe the candidate will listen to you more than to other voters. Is that fair? Does that mean your vote will count more than other voters' votes? There's a lot of disagreement about this.

By the last week of the campaign, everyone is tired. But the candidates make more speeches. They shake more hands, and they run more and more ads. Maybe, just maybe, they will convince another few voters to vote for them!

Some of these ads can be very misleading

29

Finally, it's Election Day.

Most voters are assigned a particular place to vote—a school, a library, a church basement—wherever there is space for voting booths. What if you're away on voting day? You can get an absentee ballot in advance. Some places let people vote by mail or on the Internet. A few places set up voting machines early. But however you vote, you get just one vote. You can't go back and vote again!

In most places, people use voting machines. Many cities and towns are replacing old machines with new electronic ones. But in very small towns, voters still mark paper ballots with a pencil. However you do it, you'll vote in a private booth. No one can see how you vote.

When the voting ends, the counting begins! Who will win?
Stay close to your TV or radio to find out.

Usually a few hours after the polls close, the winner is announced.

BUT WAIT!

What if the election is won by only a few votes? The candidate who lost can ask that the votes be counted again. Then it could take a few days—or longer—to carefully recount the ballots and find out who really won.

Recount? That's not fair! My mom won!

But it is fair. If I lost the election by only 105 votes, I'd ask for a recount too!

Brown wants to recount all the ballots that were mailed in.

He wants to be sure all the new voting machines were working correctly.

Do you think Chris will lose?

She might.

At last, the election is decided. In the end someone does win . . . and someone does lose.

The votes have been recounted. Bill Brown was correct. Mistakes were made . . .

. . . Smith actually has 203 votes more than Brown!

Almost half the voters don't want Chris to be mayor.

Look at the bright side. Slightly more than half DO want her!

You aren't happy? You wish the other candidate had won? Well, remember, the mayor works for everyone—even the people who didn't vote for her. She'll need to listen to *all* the voters.

After she is sworn in, the new mayor will have a few years to do her new job.

She won't please all the people all the time, but if she does a good job, maybe the voters will elect her again!

Do you know these words?

Absentee ballot—A mail-in ballot used by people who will be away on voting day.

Ballot—A sheet of paper or a card that is marked by the voter when he or she votes.

Campaign—Series of events and activities designed to help a candidate get elected

Candidate—The person who's trying to get elected.

Debate—An organized public discussion between the candidates about the issues.

Democracy—A type of government in which people choose, by voting, whom they want as their leaders and how they want their country governed.

Election—The casting of votes to decide who will hold a political office.

Independent—A person who does not join a political party.

Issues—Problems that are debated or discussed by the candidates.

Party—A group of people who join together because they share similar ideas about how the country should be governed.

Poll—A survey of people's opinions.

Polling place (or the polls)—Where voters go to vote.

Pollster (or polltaker)—A person who finds out what people are thinking.

Recount—Counting the ballots a second time because of a very close election.

This is a democracy. Anyone can run for Mayor Dog.

I'll campaign as a candidate of the Dogwaggers Party.

I'll debate the issues with the other candidate.

TIMELINE OF VOTING RIGHTS

Start here!

1776—The United States of America is born. The Declaration of Independence is signed.

The Constitution says how our country should be governed.

By 1856—Most white men can vote.

1861–65—The Civil War.

What's an amendment?

It's a change to the Constitution.

1788—Our Constitution is approved. It says it's up to each state to decide who can vote. The original 13 states say only white men who own land and pay taxes can vote. (In Pennsylvania, men just have to be taxpayers.)

1848—Seneca Falls Convention. The fight for women's rights begins, including the right to vote.

1866—Congress enacts the 14th Amendment. It says no state can deprive any person of life, liberty, or property or deny equal protection of the law.

At last!

The first woman is elected to Congress, but most women still can't vote?

This is almost 100 years after the 15th Amendment, and some people STILL can't vote?

1917—Jeannette Rankin is the first woman elected to the U.S. Congress. She is from Montana, where women can vote.

1917—Over 200 women are arrested for civil disobedience while calling for women's voting rights in a national campaign. Many are imprisoned.

1920—The 19th Amendment becomes law. Women can vote in every state!

1946–56 and 1961–65—Massive African American voter registration drives are conducted by civil rights organizations. Many new voters are registered, but there is still opposition.

The 14th Amendment didn't help much.

So another amendment was written.

But some states had "poll taxes" and difficult tests that kept blacks from voting.

1870—The 15th Amendment says that the vote shall not be denied on account of race or color.

1867—The first black voter registration drive is held.

1868—In the South, the Ku Klux Klan disrupts black voting with a campaign of terror, lynching and beating some blacks who tried to vote.

By 1913—Ten states allow women to vote: Wyoming, Colorado, Idaho, Utah, Washington, California, Arizona, Kansas, Oregon, Illinois.

This law finally solved the problem.

1789–1975! That's 186 years before everyone was able to vote.

What's in the future?

1993—The National Voter Registration Act makes it easier to register to vote.

1971—The 26th Amendment lowers the voting age to 18.

1965—The Voting Rights Act provides federal protection for African Americans who register to vote.

1975—The protections of the Voting Rights Act are extended to include Hispanic, Native American, and Asian citizens. Every citizen over age 18 can vote—except prisoners (in 46 states) and even ex-prisoners (in 10 states).

2000—There's a big problem counting votes in the presidential election, and a big disagreement over who won! What's the solution?

2002—The Help America Vote Act provides states with money to buy new voting machines and makes sure no voter is turned away and every vote is counted.

MORE ABOUT POLITICAL PARTIES

What are the two main political parties in the United States today?

The Democratic Party and the Republican Party.

What are their symbols?

The Democrats have a donkey. The Republicans have an elephant.

Are there other political parties?

Yes! The Green, Libertarian, Socialist, Independence, America First, and Reform parties have all promoted candidates in recent elections. In the past there were the Know-Nothing, Free-Soil, Bull Moose, and Whig parties—to name a few.

Do candidates have to belong to a political party?

Political parties try to help their candidates win, but there are candidates who prefer to be independent of any party.

What happens when there are candidates from more than two parties in an election?

There's a chance that none of the candidates will win more than fifty percent of the vote. If that happens, often there is another election (a runoff) between the top two vote getters. But many people think that a better solution would be for voters to rank the candidates in order of preference, indicating their first choice, their second choice, and so on. Then the candidate with the fewest votes would be eliminated and the votes counted again. What about the voters who picked the losing candidate as their first choice? Their second-choice votes would be counted. This process would be repeated until one candidate ended up with a majority of the votes—the winner! This idea is called "instant runoff."

Which parties have won presidential elections?

Between 1778 and 2007, there have been 18 Democratic, 18 Republican, 4 Whig, 2 Federalist, and 1 National Union presidents.

I'm starting the Dogwaggers Party.

The Dogwaggers' symbol will be our cat, Bubbles.

The Dogwaggers believe in soft couches, juicy bones, and Sparky for Mayor Dog

RESOURCES

Would you like to know more about voting? Here are some resources that were available when I wrote this book. For further updates, refer to my website at www.christelow.com.

www.vote-smart.org

www.loc.gov/learn/features/election

www.kidsvotingusa.org

www.archives.gov (the National Archives)

www.pbs.org/elections

www.lwv.org (the League of Women Voters)

www.fairvote.org

www.politics1.com

*Many thanks to Karen Carlson and her fourth graders
and to Michael Krasner, for their helpful comments*

Clarion Books
a Houghton Mifflin Company imprint
215 Park Avenue South, New York, NY 10003
Copyright © 2003 by Eileen Christelow
First Clarion paperback edition, 2004; reissued in 2008.
The illustrations were executed in pen and ink and acrylic gouache.
The main text was set in 17-point Magellan. The balloon text was set in Litterbox.
All rights reserved.

For information about permission to reproduce selections from this book, write to Permissions,
Houghton Mifflin Company, 215 Park Avenue South, New York, NY 10003.
www.clarionbooks.com
Manufactured in China.

The Library of Congress has cataloged the hardcover edition as follows:
Christelow, Eileen.
Vote! / Eileen Christelow.
p. cm.
Summary: Using a campaign for mayor as an example, shows the steps involved in an election,
from the candidate's speeches and rallies, to the voting booth where every vote counts, to the announcement of the winner.
ISBN 0-618-24754-8 (acid-free)
1. Voting—United States—Juvenile literature. 2. Elections—United States—Juvenile literature. 3. Political campaigns—United States—
Juvenile literature. [1. Voting. 2. Elections. 3. Politics, Practical.] I. Title.
JK1978 .C48 2003
324.973—dc21   2002152288

CL (2003) ISBN-13: 978-0-618-24754-7
PA (2004) ISBN-13: 978-0-618-48606-9
PA (2008) ISBN-13: 978-0-547-05973-0

WKT   10 9 8 7 6 5 4 3 2